# Lasting Victory

## Meditations for Students, Athletes, Coaches and Those Who Cheer Them On

# Lasting Victory

## Meditations for Students, Athletes, Coaches and Those Who Cheer Them On

*Dale Cooper*

*Kevin Vande Streek*

CALVIN ALUMNI ASSOCIATION
CALVIN COLLEGE
GRAND RAPIDS, MICHIGAN

Calvin College, Grand Rapids, Michigan 49546
© 2002 Calvin Alumni Association
All rights reserved. Published in 2002.
Printed in the United States of America

Library of Congress Control Number: 2002108271

Cooper, Dale; Vande Streek, Kevin
          Lasting Victory: Meditations for Students, Athletes,
          Coaches and Those Who Cheer Them On

ISBN 0-9703693-6-0

Cover art: from Creatas, a division of Dynamic Graphics, ©2002

# Contents

# Preface

I t's no mystery why and how we came to write this little book. Simply put:

1. We love teaching.
2. We love students.
3. We love our Lord.

Though one of us is a professor of physical education and a men's basketball coach, and the other a college chaplain and teacher of religion, our common love—yes, our passion—is teaching.

Teaching and athletics—a dynamic combination. Ever since we became colleagues at Calvin College in Grand Rapids, Michigan, several years ago, we have been discovering together that participation in sports—one of us as coach and the other as fan—has been a fine arena in which to do what we so much enjoy: to teach young people—to teach them that sound minds in sound bodies constitutes a worthy educational goal.

When God set about creating this vast universe, He crowned His efforts by fashioning human beings, creatures with the capacity to wonder, to enjoy, and to adore. Making them mirror images of Himself, God gave human beings this world as a gift. It was to be a place where they could work and labor, yes, but also where they could recreate themselves through play. God intended people to *take delight* in His creation.

But for human beings to be able to respond to His purposes, God also created them with the ability to say thanks, to be grateful for what He gave them. In and through the rhythm of our work and play, our labor alternating with our leisure, we human beings are called to give our Creator God praise: to worship and to adore Him. In order for us to become all that God intends—fully human, fully alive human beings—each of us is to become, as one theologian put it, an "echo of wonder." We are both to savor the good gifts God has given—really to revel in and to enjoy them—and also, then, to bless Him, the One who has provided these gifts.

As teachers who live and work among our college students, we have committed ourselves to live in this manner. With our Lord's help, we're aiming to cultivate the deep-down joy and delight at the sheer goodness of the gifts we have received—in this case, the gift of athletics. We want, in turn, to offer Him our appropriate and energetic gratitude. For none of us has ever deserved what we have received.

And why do we aim to live this way? First of all, because we believe that doing so gives our Lord His due. It blesses Him and gives Him greater glory.

And there's a second reason. We're passionate about modeling for our students what it means to imitate Christ and bring God honor through our individual lives. As Christian teachers we consider ourselves under charge. We have heard Jesus' open question: "When the Son of Man returns, will He find faith on the earth?" (Luke 18.8). His plain and forthright question prompts us to live our lives for the next generation in such a way that they, too, will come to believe in Jesus Christ and, then, to follow Him as Lord. We want them, in turn, eventually to transmit to their own heirs the Lord's promises and commands.

We long to do our small part, therefore, as teachers, to extend the Christian faith to the next generation. Whether as coach, as classroom instructor, as pastor, as sports fan—in all our dealings with our students—we want to be part of that innumerable company of believers whose chief passion is to live, to work, to pray, and—yes, to play!—before God's face.

We do all this to bring our Lord joy and delight.

And we do it to help shape the next generation of His children.

To the athletes and coaches who use this book:

We challenge you to set aside time to concentrate on these meditations and the questions that follow. Use this book as a journal, writing notes and responses on these pages. Be honest about the hurdles you face. Find a friend or mentor who will keep you accountable for continued spiritual growth. We know first-hand that spiritual training is a life-long pursuit which demands more dedication than any athletic endeavor. And as fellow believers and adventurers cheering you on, we encourage you to remain faithful to this pursuit, for we know that when the season of life ends for the Christian, awaiting is a crown that will last forever.

With special thanks to Dr. Steve Van Der Weele for editing these meditations, to Betsy Cooper for typing them, and to the Calvin Alumni Association for producing this book, we are,

Coach Kevin Vande Streek
Chaplain Dale Cooper

# Eyes on our Pace-Setter

*Hebrews 12.1-2*

A screaming and boisterous crowd of hometown fans, as any athlete knows, can make a world of difference to the partici-pants. Runners get their second wind, basketball players play high above the rim, and softball players deliver clutch hits, all be-cause of the loud and encouraging applause of those who are on our side. No doubt about it: warm and loyal fans are vital to an athlete's becoming a peak performer.

What drama the writer of Hebrews describes in these verses. Christians are in a dead-earnest race. But they are not going it alone. An entire company of fellow believers is applauding them and cheer-ing them on. Some are still living; others have already completed the course of their life here on earth. But all of them are joined together to spur us on in our own life's race. "Keep on keeping on," they are urging us. "We made it. So can you—if you endure."

Best of all, there is Jesus Himself at the head of the cheering mul-titude. He is, says the writer of Hebrews, both the source and goal of our faith. From Him we get power to endure. And it is toward Him that we keep running, for He is our faith's final goal.

When asked what the secret is of becoming a good tennis player, tennis great Stephen Edberg replied, "Keep your eye on the ball."

No Christian athlete will ever reach the top of her game, so to speak, without keeping her eyes upon Jesus. For Jesus—and Jesus alone—can give a Christian focus and help her to become all that she's meant to become.

## Challenge:

1. Who is part of your "cheering section" in life? Who encourages you, believes in you, and drives you to want to reach your goals?
2. In what ways are you as an athlete "looking to Jesus"?

# Nothing but the Game?

*Matthew 6.33*

E arly this summer my eye caught a middle-aged man walking down the street in Indian River, Michigan. His appearance caught my attention. Six-pack of beer cradled in his right arm and a baseball cap worn backward, he was sporting a sleeveless T-shirt which read: "Nothing Matters but the Game." Reading it, I found myself asking, "Really? Does nothing else in all of life matter? Only *the game*?"

Ask a person—any person—two simple questions: "How do you spend your time?" and "How do you spend your money?" Their answers will tell you a lot about their loyalties and priorities. If I think that, say, my studies, my relationships, my career, my hobby—or my sports—are very important, well, then I'll do and give whatever it takes to excel at them.

Some people do indeed make such activities the highest goal of their lives. They're consumed by them and gauge how worthwhile they are by their performance in them. They begin to expect not less than everything from them—life's highest gratification.

To expect too much from anything in this world is an act of idolatry. And idolatry is stupid, for none of these fleeting gratifications can satisfy the deepest cravings and longings God has planted in our hearts.

Sports can be a great and good part of our lives; they never should become our god.

Our Lord's life is very instructive here: He lived for His Father alone—and for His Father's kingdom. He longed to do His Father's will: to follow His Father's commands and to enjoy His Father's promises. His greatest delight was to bring His Father pleasure. He was eager to live—and willing to die—for the sake of His Father's kingdom.

Jesus encourages us as athletes to keep our priorities straight. We may rightfully play, of course, and play hard while we're doing it. But not simply because "life is short," as Nike ads say. Rather, we play in such a way that we show that nothing finally matters but our Lord's kingdom. And bringing our Father joy as we play.

Because more matters in life than merely the game.

A lot more.

## Challenge:

Spend some time alone. Ask yourself some vital questions:

1. What is the highest purpose, the deepest desire, of my life?
2. How does my life as an athlete fit in with my highest goal?
3. What idol might I be clinging to in my life?
4. Who is holding me accountable to living with proper balance?

# Playing Hard for a Crowd of One

*Colossians 3.23-24, I Thessalonians 4.1*

One of my friends, Andrea, an All-American javelin thrower, forwarded to me an E-mail message her father sent her during an especially trying time in her quest to get to the NCAA Nationals. Here's what he wrote her:

"In terms of javelin throwing: God gave you an ability. When you throw, I can assure you He isn't focused on how many inches or feet you are short of your goals. Rather, He is saying to His angels, 'Hey, look, there's My Andrea throwing again. Look how she's developed over the years. She's got a smooth approach, and she's got the mechanics down. Look how gracefully she performs. What a beautiful picture!'

"If you make it to the Nationals, it will be because He wants you there—probably not for how well you might do, but because there are people there who need your encouraging word, your testimony, or your care. As far as the actual throwing goes, throw to please Him— you've got an audience of One."

Olympic sprinter Eric Liddell (featured in the movie *Chariots of Fire*) said: "God made me fast. And when I run, I feel His pleasure."

**For you to consider**:
1. When God looks at you perform, how does He judge you?
2. What can you do to increase God's pleasure as you compete?

# God's Playground

*Psalm 8*

Compared to the size of the universe and to the God who made it all, each of us is incredibly tiny. For every single human being God ever made, He also made more than 2.4 *trillion* stars. Even with only a limited awareness of this immensity, the Psalmist asks, "What is a man"—or even all human beings put together—"that You, O Lord, are mindful of him?" No matter who we are, and no matter how important we judge ourselves to be, at one level we're no big deal, really.

In another sense, however, we're a profoundly big deal. For God created this vast universe and gave it to each of us *as a gift*. A *personal* gift, I might add, crafted especially for us, the creatures in whom He takes special delight. God made each of us a "little lower than the angels" and crowned us with glory and honor.

In doing all this for us, God is saying to each of us, in effect: "Go ahead, enjoy yourselves. To be sure, take what you do seriously. But at the same time, don't take *yourself* too seriously. For the truth is that each of you is—wonderfully—a little child at play on My vast playground."

As coach I've often told my players: "Work hard, have fun, and success will take care of itself." We spend time on scouting reports about our opponent, and on major things like offensive entries and defensive systems. Then we hammer away at the smaller details—

opening jump ball, inbounding the ball, deflections, and loose ball recoveries.

Amid our diligence, however necessary, it is very possible to lose something precious and important: the sheer joy of the game.

An appropriate question for each of us to ask, again and again, is this: "Are we still having fun?" For God created us—and Jesus saved us—so that we might have *joy*—deep-down delight in His immense gifts to us.

Try this. The next time you put on your spikes or step to the starting line, before you suit up for the game or take the field for batting practice, think of yourself as a little child who is about to step onto God's playground.

Then go out and play. Play to your heart's delight. Play like a child. For that is what you really are.

**To Ask Yourself**:
1. Take the measure of what you think about yourself: How big and important do you think you are? And how little?
2. Are you *enjoying* your life as an athlete? Are you having fun?

# A Minor Detail, A Major Difference

*Romans 8.35-39*

In one of his novels, writer/preacher Frederick Buechner records a scene in which Antonio Parr returns home after a long time away. Wanting to give him a deep and warm welcome, his children hang a banner up on the garage door. It reads: "Welcome ho*ne*." Comments Buechner: "It was a mere stroke (of the pen), a minor serif. But," he added, "sometimes a minor stroke can make a major difference."

How often the difference between winning or losing a game is so very thin—a matter of inches or of a single play. A poor inbounds pass, a bases-loaded strikeout in the bottom of the ninth, a fumble, a disputable call—any one of these can mean a game lost.

So, too, with the good things that happen. In an adrenalin-flowing, nail-biting finish to the all-conference track meet, someone runs her PR-best in the final leg of the 4x400. The result: her team wins—both the meet and also the league crown. Or, again, a desperation 35-foot buzzer-beater hits nothing but net—and our team wins by a single point.

Consider, too, all the fine-print details of what may happen to us as athletes—the freak but crippling injuries, the awards, the unexplained dips in performance, the illnesses.

A couple of years ago, before the regular season even had begun, a veteran basketball player, while crashing the boards for a rebound, got a finger in his eye. He was out, of course, for the rest of the game; far worse, he faced the real danger of losing his sight permanently.

Taken by itself, the accident was a minor detail, a tiny happening. But it could have made a major difference.

Amid all of these happenings, both potential and actual, the vital question for us athletes is this: How do we view these little happenings? What is our attitude toward them? Do they frustrate us, get us down, overwhelm us and kill our joy? Or do we view ourselves as players who are being held in the careful embrace of a big God? A God to Whom—amid the vast multitude of the little events that happen to us—we are very precious.

St. Paul knew that trust in this big God is the key to tranquility, comfort, and courage. For he was confident that nothing—simply nothing—could separate him from the love of God.

If we, too, as Paul did, work on cultivating our own trust and reliance upon this big God—as much and as hard as we work on other parts of our game—then we'll be able to handle the joys and disappointments—all of them—which come our way.

*If.*

## Questions:
1. How do you handle successes as an athlete? Failures?
2. What will it take for you to cultivate trust in a big God?

# God's Longing

*Ephesians 1.1-5*

N o doubt about it: God takes a deep and warm interest in all
the things that happen to us. After all, He made us with ex-
quisite care and attention. Scripture describes God as our
Father and us as His children.

If you know from experience how good it feels to have a parent,
a grandparent, a friend, or a guardian who loves and cares about you,
who comes to watch you play and who's your chief fan, well, try
multiplying that by infinity. Only then will you catch a faint hint of
how much interest God your heavenly Father takes in your life as an
athlete. He *loves* to watch you compete.

Above all else, however, God has in mind one other accomplishment for you. Even more than taking delight in watching you grow
into the finest athlete you can be, God desires you to become like
Jesus. He is eager that you grow in your love for Jesus. He wants you,
too, to act more and more like Jesus. For, as God's first-born Son,
Jesus models for us how to live in order to please God.

To put matters in a single word, God wants you to become
"holy"—to become a saint. It's quite simple to explain what a saint is,
really, but to become one takes a lifetime of diligent focus and practice. We expect you as students to become saintly scholars, educated
believers. Now add athletics to the formula, and you really have a
daunting challenge. It's harder than any drill or practice that any

coach has ever thought of putting you through. Every day it takes God's power and help to become such a person.

But no matter how difficult the task, saints strive diligently to conform to the image of Christ Himself. They never tire of asking what Jesus would do if He were in their shoes. They try to shape their motives and ambitions, their speech and actions, by the example He set.

Nor is there ever an off-season. Every day God our Father keeps sending us "stuff" for us to train and practice on. The people we meet, the choices He sets before us, and all the things that happen to us—each of these God intends as the raw material for us to become like Jesus.

### Challenge:

Pause for a few moments, and pay attention to your life. Find a specific area where you need to grow more toward becoming like Jesus. What will you do about it? Who will hold you accountable?

# God is Big—When We're Victors

*Psalm 100*

n sports, nothing's more fun than winning. But when success does come, how ought *Christian* athletes to handle it? I'd like to suggest that we cultivate joy—Christian joy.

Joy comes when we appreciate that these good things—in this case, winning—are gifts.

And to understand the best way to receive a gift, you have to watch how little children do it.

Suppose it's a five-year-old's birthday. You've bought him a gift, brightly wrapped it, and put a bow on top. You then release it from your hands and put it into his, along with a strong "Happy Birthday!" What does he do? How does he respond? Well, he holds the gift for the briefest of moments; he shakes it, trying to guess what's inside; and then, wide-eyed with eager wonder, he rips the paper off. If what's inside is something he really has wanted for so long—has dreamed about for weeks—he'll jump up and down, exclaiming with delight: "I *got* it!"

And then, if he's polite, he'll do one more thing. He will turn to you, the giver, and say, with a big and warm smile: "Thank you. Thank you so much!"

If you pay careful attention to what happened—the sequence of giving, receiving, and thanking—you'll get a fine glimpse about how to handle your victories and successes in sports. Everything—simply *everything* you have gotten, including your successes—is a gift from God. You never deserved these gifts—at least certainly no more than anybody else.

How does God the Giver wish you to respond? Well, like small children do—be captured by the wonder of it all. So jump up and down, high-five one another, do somersaults—whatever it takes to make you become wide-eyed and kid-like again. For God joins you in the joy—He *loves* it, too, when He sees His children having a good time.

And please do one more thing: Tell Him your thanks for what He's given. It's not only a polite thing to do. It's so right and fitting. For it is He Who has given you the joyful delight of winning the contest.

Just think of it: A sheer gift—and to you!

## Challenge:

Remember the most successful event in your athletic career—your highest accomplishment, your favorite win. Savor it again. And then thank the Giver for it.

# God is Big—Even When We're Losers

*Psalm 138.7-8, II Corinthians 12*

N o athlete wins all of the time. Not Michael or Tiger, not Martina or Serena.

Nor you.

Losing is really hard, of course, and when defeat comes, how do you—as a Christian—handle it? How *ought* you to?

Let's begin with how *not* to. Let me suggest three things to avoid: frustration, resentment, and fear. Frustration is the tendency to belittle yourself, to knock yourself down by saying—perhaps over and over again: "I could have done better. I *should have* done better. How *stupid and idiotic* of me not to have done better!"

Frustration helps no one, of course—neither you nor your teammates nor coaches. Worst of all, it is displeasing to God; He hates to see you killing your own joy. Practicing frustration only makes you, well, more and more frustrated.

Resentment means cultivating hate—perhaps toward yourself, perhaps toward a specific member of your team or the entire team itself, or, maybe, toward the coaches and fans—for what went wrong. You begin to let bitterness sprout deep within your soul; you continue feeding it little by little. And the next thing you know, you simply can't *stand* the one you've allowed yourself to resent. That's bad for your mental health. Resentment also disappoints our Lord.

Fear, too, can burrow its way into our spirits after we've suffered a loss. We begin to brood about it. We play it over and over again in our minds, making it a larger matter than it should be.

And, then, worst of all, we go on to think we'll never get over it. We'll *never* conquer it, we'll never win again, we'll never see happiness again. You know how fear works: it paralyzes you.

What's the Christian antidote? It's trust. Trust in a big God Who's got the world in His hands, including each of us when we lose. We belong to Him, and He loves us unconditionally.

Even when we're at rock bottom, and think we'll never rise again, He loves us still.

### Challenge:

Remember your worst loss, your worst mistake—the moment in your career when you felt the lowest. How did you respond? Could your response have been better and more pleasing to God?

# God is Big—When We're Injured

*Psalm 138; II Corinthians 12*

osing a key game is hard. But it's nothing compared to an injury or an illness that cuts short your season—or your career. In that single "awful instant" all of your dreams and hopes, all of your ambitions and desires come crashing down. At times it seems almost too bad to be true. "It can't be happening," we find ourselves saying. But, sad to say, it can be.

If such a tragedy should happen to you—let's hope that it never will, but reckon that, yes, it could—how then will you respond?

Pay attention to the response of a young woman—my own mother, Marjorie Cooper. She was cut down in the prime of her life. At 26 she became totally paralyzed from her neck down. She ended up living that way for 40 years longer.

When her illness first happened, she couldn't take it in. Life seemed not worth living. She begged God to die. But, gradually, inch by little inch, she endured. And amid her terrible distress, she learned to be quiet enough to listen to God. He spoke directly to her troubled heart and anxious spirit.

Here, so she said, is what God kept telling her:

1. "Don't look back to yesterday with an attitude of 'If only it hadn't happened.' It *did* happen. Wishing things were otherwise won't make them change."

2. "Don't look to tomorrow—and to a long string of seemingly

endless tomorrows after that—with an anxious 'What if…?' Doing so only produces worry upon worry."

3. "Trust me just for today—for the next span of 24 hours. If you do, I'll promise you enough strength to endure."

And the result? She discovered that God was being faithful to what He had promised. He was breathing fresh strength into her spirit day by day. And in the long, transforming process my mother eventually became anything but a victim of the dread disease which paralyzed her body. Clearly, she became victor over it.

With our Lord beside us, no matter what may happen to us, we're always on the winning side.

*Always.*

## Challenge:

Are there areas of your life as an athlete in which God is calling you to trust Him more and more? Identify them, and then pray: "Lord, I surrender (envy, one-upmanship, impatience, whatever) to you. Be faithful to me as You promise You will."

# On Setting Goals

*Philippians 3.12-14; Acts 20.24*

"The roads to nowhere are hard to make. For a person to work well, there has to be an end in view." That was the comment of a historian about those who, during the American Depression of the 1930s, were put to work doing useless tasks—like building roads that served no real and good purpose. These workers couldn't get motivated, for the tasks they were performing were exercises in futility.

The historian's comment is true about us all. No one can really give something her best shot—her most passionate and emotional "everything"—unless she knows that it is serving a good purpose, a higher goal.

Keeping our goals in mind can help us maintain our focus and keep us rallied around a common cause. Vision ought always to inform our strategy, and strategy, in turn, ought to give shape to our program.

But the whole process begins with vision—with goals. A team without goals is like 15 dogs on bungee cords.

For a Christian athlete, no personal or team goals are really worthwhile unless he knows that they serve a higher cause. Unless they flow out of and contribute to what pleases his Lord Jesus and enhances God's kingdom, these goals resemble a cul-de-sac.

A Christian athlete, therefore, tries to remember that he is a very tiny player in a much larger game—a small contributor to a much larger cause, the cause of Christ.

St. Paul is a good example of one who was focused, who gave not less than everything toward "the goal to win the prize for which God has called me heavenward in Christ Jesus." For Jesus Paul was willing to die; for Jesus he was eager to continue to live. Jesus' kingdom was the goal of his life—nothing more, nothing less, nothing else.

## Challenge:

Meditate on Acts 20.24. Then write out your own physical, mental, emotional, relational, and spiritual goals. Check how each of them contributes to your overall goal to live for Jesus Christ.

# In the Quest for Excellence
# There is No Finish Line

*Acts 20.24; Romans 12.1-2*

L egendary UCLA basketball coach John Wooden once commented, "You must be willing to sacrifice what you are for what you can become." It was his way of addressing the tendency in athletes to become content with their performance, to slack off and lose passion for the game. They begin to give, as I saw on the T-shirt of a Chicago marathoner last fall, "only 109 percent." They give a little bit less than their best effort for every game.

A Christian athlete, in response to his Lord who gave His everything for him, never stops striving to improve in all aspects of his game. And he does so gladly, not grudgingly, for he keeps in mind what his Lord has so willingly done for him.

So a charged and motivated Christian athlete will do whatever it takes. If it means coming in early and staying late in order to sharpen his skills and improve his game, he'll do it—no question about it. Never—simply never—will he settle for "just getting by." "Just enough" isn't good enough.

In the spiritual life, too, "resting content" and "doing just enough" can become a problem. Time and again throughout Scripture we read of God's people who gave Him less than their finest. They gave God their blemished lambs, their cheapest grain, their bare minimum of ten percent. And even then they did so grudgingly.

St. Paul pleads: "Therefore, I urge you, people of God, *in view of what God has done,* to present yourselves as living sacrifices of thanks to Him" (Rom. 12.1).

Paul himself was an example of this determined drive to give himself more and more fully. He said about himself, "I consider my life worth nothing, except that I may win the race and complete the course which the Lord Jesus has assigned to me, to testify to the gospel of His grace."

### Questions:

1. Where in your athletic performance do you need to improve? How much of yourself are you willing to surrender to do so?
2. Where do you need to grow spiritually? Check the level of your willingness, your desire to do so.

# Who Are You? What Are Your Gifts?

*Romans 12.4-8*

An important part of being an athlete is knowing what kind of player you are. To be able to assess your strengths and weaknesses is important to knowing where you can make your biggest contribution to the team.

"Know thyself," said the Greek philosopher Socrates. That's good advice for everyone—for athletes, too. If you are to make a significant contribution to your team, you must honestly appraise your strengths and your weaknesses. Moreover, an entire team must come to know a coach's strengths and weaknesses, too, so that—together—they can work on becoming the finest they can be.

It's so obvious: on a team each of us will contribute in a different way. Our gifts vary, but everyone is important—crucial, even. While one type of gift may attract more attention and generate more applause, each one is vital.

Christian athletes gladly acknowledge the diversity of gifts on a team. They know the contribution that they themselves can make, but they are also generous in recognizing others' gifts. They know how dependent they are on a wide range of abilities.

In Christ's kingdom, too, we all have different gifts "according to the grace given" (Rom. 12.6). God has distributed among Christ's disciples a wide array of distinct abilities—unique talents that each of us can use to bless, serve, and enrich the others. Together we form Christ's body, a living organism in which each member plays a vital role.

Nor is there any gradation, in God the Giver's eyes, in the importance of the gifts. Each is equal in value to the rest. The gift of hospitality, for example, is as necessary and as beautiful as the gift of contributing to the needs of others.

In Christ's beautiful body, therefore, no one may downplay her own or another's gift. For each is important. And God has distributed these gifts as it has pleased Him.

In March, 2000, the Calvin College men's basketball team won the national championship. When the announcer called the tri-captains to come out on the floor to receive the trophy, these three men spontaneously—yes, automatically—motioned for the entire rest of the team to join them. This gesture symbolized the unity of spirit which had characterized the team all season.

When I saw the eager gestures of welcome from these three young men, inviting the rest of their team to join them at center court, I caught a tiny glimpse, a visible parable, of the kingdom of God.

## Challenge:

What can you contribute to your team? What can you receive from your fellow team members?

# Self-Esteem 101

*Ephesians 2.10, Psalm 139*

S ome athletes hang a lot on how well they and their team do. They wrap their whole sense of identity and of worthwhileness around their performance. If they do well, their self-esteem soars. If they don't, everything else begins to tumble and crash. They get down on themselves, considering themselves mediocre or worse.

Some athletes peg their own value by comparing their performance to others. If their times are faster, if they hurl faster, if they gain a starting position over all their rivals, if their stats are better than everyone else's, then they begin to feel good about themselves. But if others begin to surpass them, they berate, insult, and condemn themselves. In fact, they begin to do a little murder on themselves.

If you base your sense of self-esteem only upon your performance, you're guaranteed to lose. Always.

And you know why, of course. Because the farther you go on in sports, the greater the chance that you're going to come up against someone who is better than you are. In junior high, you may have been the big athlete in school. But by the time you get to college, you'll discover that you're pretty marvelously average, really. Performance-based self-esteem is bound to kill one's joy. Sooner or later, everyone—*everyone*—gets his come-uppance.

Performance-based mentality seems to be everywhere nowadays. Look, for example, at the signs people hold up at important games:

"We're the greatest," and "We're #1." As though losing and being #2 mean that you're worth nothing!

An athlete who tries to follow Christ and to bring Him honor will be on the alert for this sick and evil tendency, this clever temptation of the devil. With his Lord's help, he'll pull it out by the roots. He knows, deep down, that his value as a person and athlete doesn't depend upon the outcome of the game or upon how well he does. Rather, his value is anchored to a far more secure foundation. It is grounded in a God who created him and in a Savior who has saved him. Secure in the knowledge that he knows he belongs finally and fully to God—and to God alone—he can play hard, yes, and have great fun doing so. And then, with the game over, he can rest.

And rest well.

**Challenge**:

Check your inner life. Where does your sense of self-esteem and security lie: in yourself or in your God?

# Superstars or Super-egos?

*Philippians 2.5-11*

Some people do great things and, to their surprise, become famous. Others do little, but they try strenuously to have that little become a basis for fame. Sometimes that works—temporarily. We call them celebrities. The difference between the "surprised by fame" folk and the celebrity-status seekers is enormous.

An athlete who bears Christ's name might eventually become famous; she ought never to become a celebrity. For a Christian declares continually her *dependence,* not her independence.

In the first place, a Christian athlete has an appropriate sense of humility toward her Lord. She knows that all that she has achieved and hopes yet to become as an athlete is a sheer gift from God, something that she hasn't earned or deserved. Continually she practices saying thanks to Him.

Then, too, a Christian athlete is humble toward others. Never will she try to make herself look better at others' expense. She is quick with a good word about others, not about herself.

In all of this the Christian athlete is imitating Jesus her Lord. For, though great, He was willing to become lower than all of us. He took the form of a servant, and gave His life for us.

Cultivating humility is never easy. Says one of Calvin College's finest athletes, an All-American: "One of the hardest things for athletes to accomplish in sports is to be good and be humble at the same time."

Doing so, however, is mandatory. Doing so is to become Christ-like. Doing so is to give our Lord the glory, and not to snatch it for ourselves.

**Questions:**

1. How do you declare your dependence on Christ through your words and actions?
2. What can you do to cultivate humility in your life?

# Blueprints for Success: Positive Mental Attitude

*Proverbs 3.26*

F ormer New York Yankee catcher, the inimitable Yogi Berra, remembered as much off the field for his awkward expressions of speech as he is for his great playing on it, said one time, "Ninety percent of the game is half-mental."

So much of success in sports depends upon the level of a player's confidence. Take basketball, for example. If a player gets into a slump, in his mind he begins *hoping*—desperately!—that the ball will go through the hoop rather than *knowing*—for sure—that it's going through.

A positive mental attitude is so hard to define. But when it's present, a team can play high above the rim. And when it's not, well, the team is merely unusually average.

How do you get a positive mental attitude back once it's oozed away? First, don't take yourself too seriously. Lighten up. Resist the tendency to hammer on yourself about what you might be doing wrong. Sometimes the more you focus on "How badly I'm doing" and "I'm not confident enough," the less confident you become. Just focus on the joy of the game.

Then try some extra practice. For example, if it's poor free-throw shooting that's paralyzing you with fear, work on getting your rhythm back. Practice, practice, practice.

The same advice holds true for our lives as Christians. The Evil One desires to put us in a spiritual slump—to doubt God, to kill your joy in Christ, to question whether you're doing right by following His will. The best defense against him is a good offense. Keep doing what you know can restore your confidence in God and deliver you from your spiritual slump. Don't beat up on your mind and spirit, again and again, with how much you're doubting. That will only make matters worse. Rather, simply pray, quietly and longingly, for your awareness of our Lord's presence to return. And then keep doing what you know will nourish you and restore your confidence: Read God's Word faithfully and meditate upon His promises to you.

God has written these promises in His Word for you. He longs to breathe them into your slumping, tired spirit. He wants your spirit to sing again.

### Questions:

What spiritual exercises do you practice to thrive as a Christian? How regularly do you do them?

# Blueprints for Success: Enthusiasm

*II Peter 1.5; Nehemiah 8.10*

S everal years ago a high-school senior, a good student academically, a strong running back on his football team, a leader in his church youth group, kind and polite to everyone—simply put, a fine young man and so full of promise—was killed in an auto accident. He was hit by a drunk driver. He was the nerve center of his team, one who by his words and actions could rally his team and make it play at peak performance.

After he died, the team's coach called his players together. He challenged them to "play for Devon"—to remember their fallen teammate and to let the memory of him inspire their play. Thus, prior to each game the team huddled to recall Devon. Mainly, they told stories, sometimes laughing and at other times weeping as they recalled memories of what they had accomplished with Devon and how he had inspired them.

Then, in an act which soon took on the air and importance of a ritual, together they put on armbands with Devon's initials on them. The team captain's final words to his team before they took the field were, "Play hard tonight. Play with Devon in you."

St. Peter wrote his words to a group of young Christians who had become worn and tired in their faith. Their spirits weren't magnetically exciting, full of contagious joy, as they should have been. So, he rouses them to "make every effort"—thus, make it a top priority—to "add to your faith." He lists a number of attitudes to practice—qualities which will get them out of their slump and help their spirits to sing again. The first of them is "goodness," translated sometimes as "enthusiasm."

"Enthusiasm" means "inspired by, or possessed by, God." The term reveals an important New Testament claim about us: God, through Christ, dwells within us, and we are in Him. St. Paul never tires of reminding the early believers of this astonishing truth. No fewer than 164 times in his 13 letters, in fact, he states that they are "in the Lord" and that Christ is "in us."

Thus, it's not merely true that Jesus our Lord is *for* us. He is that, of course. But equally important, and perhaps more so, He also is *in* us. His Spirit's presence and power dwell within us—literally—and give us energy, when we perform as athletes, to play our game with *enthusiasm*—with the sense of charged excitement and joy.

A dull, half-hearted Christian athlete is oxymoronic—simply impossible. For Christ is living within us. Hence, our challenge: "Remember Christ. Play with Christ in you."

**Challenge:**

Read Philippians 1.21 and Colossians 1.27. How do these truths shape you as an athlete?

# Blueprints for Success: Knowledge

*II Peter 1.5-7*

D eveloping a good game plan and then executing it with precision, as any athlete knows, are vital to defending against an opponent. Coming up with a good strategy to contain the opponent requires intelligence. Both coaches and players have to think hard about the opposing team's strengths and weaknesses as well as their own. And then they must plan accordingly.

So, too, in one's spiritual life. St. Peter advises that the second ingredient for conquering spiritual slump is "knowledge." In this case, he means doing a cool and very calculated reckoning about how the Evil One operates, and then coming up with an appropriate strategy to oppose him.

Temptations come personally crafted by the devil. Therefore, to do battle with the devil, one ought to do three things: Know oneself; know one's tempter, and know one's temptations.

1. *Know oneself.* That is, know how weak and vulnerable you are to withstand temptations. Acknowledge this about yourself. Never mistakenly think that you, too, couldn't tumble into the same sins where others have already fallen. That's foolish. Remember, pride goes before a damaging fall.

2. *Know one's tempter.* Reckon seriously with how crafty he is, and how powerful. Never underestimate the strength of your spiritual opponent, the Evil One.

3. *Know one's temptations.* Not all of us are vulnerable in the same way. Some find one kind of sinning harder to withstand than others do. Satan is aware of your "soft spots," your weak areas. He's no fool: he lobs his temptations toward these weak spots with pinpoint accuracy.

Wise Christians develop solid spiritual game plans. And the first point in their strategy is always this: Ask the Lord Jesus—Whom Satan can never outwit or conquer—for help in the spiritual battle.

Depending on Christ your Lord, you need never lose.

### Questions:

In what area of your life are you especially weak and tempted? What strategy are you using to withstand the Evil One in this area?

# Blueprints for Success:
# Self-Discipline, Self-Control

*II Peter 1.5-7*

How many times doesn't it happen: A player makes a mistake—he misses a shot, commits an infield error, throws an interception—and, in response, he does something stupid. He loses his cool and in frustration commits yet another error. The explanation is simple: He's lost control of himself.

A Christian athlete strives to practice "self-control." Control over one's own person is the third character-quality which St. Peter encourages followers of Jesus Christ to practice. It acts like a watch-guard at a gate. It inspects thoroughly; it takes careful account. It refuses to allow simply anyone and everything into one's life, because it reckons with the fact that—to put it bluntly—some responses and attitudes are not good for a person. In fact, they're dangerously bad. Once inside, they can do awful damage.

Self-control knows, too, how temptations work: seeing with one's physical eyes or hearing with one's ears leads one to imagine. Imagining, in turn, leads a person to act. Actions eventually become habits. Habits become stuff by which charachter gets formed. And, finally, character shapes one's destiny.

Because doing evil is so addictive and habit-forming, self-control tries to keep temptation from even getting a start.

A Christian athlete strives for self-control both on and off the field. She watches carefully what mental images she allows into her life. For she knows that these mental expeditions are vital to her growing into the woman God wants her to become.

## Challenge:

Recall a time when you lost your cool. What did you learn from it? How could you have handled it differently?

# Blueprints for Success: Perseverance

*II Peter 1.5-7*

Sacrifice, dedication, desire, endurance, perseverance: none of these words bring to mind ease, or pleasantness, or fun. To persevere means that you don't swerve from the path when the wind is hard in your face and not at your back.

Perseverance is crucial to any athlete's success. Mastery of a sport comes after long and determined perseverance: dogged and diligent effort during practice times, and going all-out, from start to finish, during the competition itself. No great athlete just "happened" into greatness. It takes drive and heavy sacrifice—determined hard work— no matter what might stand in the way.

Football coach Lou Holtz said one time: "Success is obtained by uncommon people willing to do what the common people won't do. If what you did yesterday still looks big, you haven't done anything today."

To live the Christian life requires perseverance, too. In fact, Scripture often compares the Christian life to an endurance race. St. Paul says: "Everyone who competes in the games goes into strict training.... Therefore I do not run like a man running aimlessly; I do not fight like a man beating the air. No, I beat my body and make it my slave so that ... I myself will not be disqualified for the prize" (I Cor. 9.25-27).

You know it from experience: Wind sprints are never fun. Sometimes you think you're going to die from exhaustion. But when you refuse to quit and actually do finish, then you discover that you have become much better prepared physically and mentally for a rough game. Because you know that you've *paid your dues* to be where you are.

The same holds true spiritually. Be confident of this: When we depend upon God for strength to do so, then the promise is true: "He who endures to the end will be saved."

**Questions:**

What is your "perseverance level" as an athlete? How much are you giving in order to succeed? How about in your spiritual life?

# Blueprints for Success: Godliness

*II Peter 1.5-7*

Think of a person in your life—a parent, a teacher, a coach, any one—who means not less than everything to you. When her name gets mentioned, your spine tingles with excitement and joy. You're willing to do whatever she may require of you—without blinking or questioning—because she has already done so much for you. You trust her advice. You imitate her actions. In fact, you long to be just like her. You love this person.

Multiply such thoughts and emotions by infinity, and you get a faint hint of what St. Peter means by "godliness." The term connotes a combination of awe and reverence toward God—even fear of Him. But not a cringing fear, a paralyzing fright. On the contrary, it's a fear caused by His *goodness*. He's so good to us, in fact, that our jaws open wide and our eyes fill with wonder when we pause to think of all that He is and all that He's done for us.

Because He's radically different from any one of His creatures—because God is God, and we are not—He does not allow us to speak about Him frivolously or without due respect. He is holy. But who, after all, would even think about doing so, considering how exalted He is, and how small and insignificant we are in comparison? Would one even think of dragging, let's say, her beloved coach into disrespect by flippantly tossing her name around?

Awe and respect toward God—the quality of "godliness"—produces a desire to both worship and serve Him: worship because of who He is and because of what He has done, and service, because it pleases our Lord and is our way of showing Him our thanks.

Every aspect of our entire life, including our life as an athlete, can become an instrument to both worship and serve our God—to honor Him for who He is, and to express our thanks for what He's done.

So, the next time you step to the plate or get ready to hurl the javelin or before you get set for the jump ball or take your racket in hand, pause for a moment. Bless God for His being God—your God—and then dedicate your play to Him.

Live—and play—your godliness everywhere you go.

It's the right thing to do.

For God, after all, is God.

# Blueprints for Success:
# Brotherly Kindness

*II Peter 1.5-7*

One of my favorite parts of a game occurs when one player shows kindness to his opponent—gives him an approving smile, helps him off the floor, pats him on the butt after a hard foul. To be sure, such a gesture isn't required—and it is expected even less. It's simply a classy thing to do.

My friend and fellow coach, Rick Temple, was recently diagnosed with leukemia. He needed not only a bone marrow transplant but also weeks and months of therapy. These treatments, plus a lot of money to have them done.

Rick told me of the heavy shower of kindnesses which so many people poured out on him during this difficult season of his life. But nothing meant more to him, or touched him so much, as the warm and thoughtful gesture of an opposing team of eighth-grade players. These boys passed the hat among themselves and publicly presented their offering to Rick when his team played theirs at their gym.

To be kind: it's not a wimpy thing to do. It takes strength. It sets leaders off from average folk. It is Christ-like.

**Challenge:**

1. Measure your kindness-level: When is the last time you did something kind—a courtesy for a team member, for your coach, for the trainer, for the custodian, for your parents, or for an opposing player?
2. Think of something kind to say or do today. Then do it.

# Blueprints for Success: Love

*II Peter 1.5-7*

I n his book *Love Beyond Reason* John Ortberg describes Pandy, the beloved doll of his grown sister, Barbie. An aunt gave it to Barbie on her birthday when she was young. Pandy went everywhere with Barbie. Barbie loved Pandy "with a love that was too strong for Pandy's own good."

Over time Pandy lost her outward attractiveness: Her hair got pulled out, one of her arms was torn off, some of the stuffing got knocked out of her.

On a family trip one time Barbie accidentally left Pandy in a hotel room high in northern Canada. She realized it when the family was nearly back home in Rockford, Illinois. With no hesitation, Barbie's father made a U-turn and went all the way back to reclaim that precious doll. Comments Ortberg: "The measure of my sister's love for that doll was that she would travel all the way to a distant country to save her."

This episode in the life of Barbie and Pandy gives us a good glimpse into the nature of St. Peter's term for love—*agape*. Agape doesn't calculate the cost of loving; it simply gives—and gives again. And again—no matter how long, and come what may.

Agape is God's kind of love. It's what moved Him to send Jesus to save us.

In response to His love toward us, God calls us to show agape. We show it first toward Him ("Love the Lord your God...."), and then toward others ("Love your neighbor as yourself") (Matt. 22.37-39).

Jesus adds: "Whatever you did for one of the least of these... you did for Me" (Matt. 25.40). How much we love others, no matter how unlovable they might be, is a direct measure of how much we love our Lord.

As an athletic season comes to a close, nearly everyone feels a deep sense of sadness. The finality grips us: the last time in the stadium, the last time with our teammates in the locker room, the last playing of the National Anthem, the last time for the seniors. Even the iciest athlete tends to get emotional. For we begin to sense how much we care about one another—how much we have come to *love* one another.

Christian athletes remind themselves and one another about the source of this bond of love: God's supreme love for us in Christ.

And for this love—His love toward them, and theirs back toward Him and toward one another in response—they never tire of saying thanks.

### Questions:
1. Do you regularly say thank-you to God for the people you love?
2. Is there someone you are having difficulty loving? Ask God to fill your heart with agape love for this person.

# Achieving Peak Performance: Worship

*Psalms 29, 103*

Much like going to the doctor for an annual checkup on your body, it's good to do a regular checkup on your soul. You need now and then to hold a spiritual stethoscope close to your heart, so to speak, and to listen carefully to how well it's pumping spiritual nourishment to your entire person. Your heart, the very spirit and center of who you are, is a vast storehouse of thoughts, attitudes, emotions, desires, and drives; each one of these can quickly become diseased. The result: Your entire person gets affected and begins to suffer.

Good doctors know what questions to ask their patients. Spiritual doctors, too. Here, says Gordon MacDonald, is a good one to start a spiritual diagnosis: "Whom am I really trying to please?" That is, "Whose good thought about myself do I value most?"

In his spiritual journal, *The Confessions*, St. Augustine (4th century) prayed to God: "O Lord, our hearts are restless until they rest in You. *For we were made for You*" (italics mine). Another time-tested statement of faith, the Westminster Confession (17th century), declares clearly and boldly: "The chief goal of man is to bring glory to God and to enjoy Him forever."

We were made to worship and adore. God our Maker has placed within our hearts a never-ceasing drive to bring Him His due glory and honor. Healthy souls, therefore, respond eagerly to the inviting command of the Psalmist: "Ascribe to the Lord glory and honor" (Ps. 29.1) and "Praise the Lord, O my soul; all my inmost being, praise His holy name. Praise the Lord and forget not all His benefits" (Ps. 103.1-2).

Sick and sinful people that we are, however, time and again we discover ourselves wandering off to worship other—lesser—gods. For example, we begin to crave the applause and approval of friends so much that we make it our top priority in life to please them. Or, again, the good smile of a coach comes to mean more to us than anything else, so we live for it. Still, again, the thought about winning the championship starts to creep into our minds—ever so softly, gently and infrequently at first—but quite soon it becomes all we can think about. We simply *must* have that huge ring on our finger to *prove* that "We're number one!"

When her soul is healthy and working properly, a Christian athlete is prompted every day to exclaim: "Not to me, not to me, O Lord, but to Your name be the glory, because of Your steadfast love and faithfulness to me" (Ps. 115.1).

In other words, it is You, O Lord, that I long to please. And it is for Your greater honor and glory—and Yours alone—that I long to play and live.

**Questions:**

As an athlete, for whom are you really living? Whom are you trying to please?

# Achieving Peak Performance: Prayer

*I Thessalonians 5.17; Psalm 62*

G ood communication among team members, as every athlete knows, is vital to a team's success. Fine team play depends upon it. When it's present, a team can accomplish extraordinary feats. When it's not, things fall apart, no matter how good each of the individual players might be.

The same is true in our spiritual life. A healthy, breathing soul maintains communication with God. Prayer is the air it breathes.

Good prayer is a two-way conversation. It begins with God's speaking and our listening. He is more important than we are, and His speech to us is more important than anything we might say to Him. Therefore, we must learn to listen.

*Learn* to listen, I say, for listening is by no means an easy thing to do. The Psalmist discovers that he must rouse his soul and command it to listen: "My soul, wait in silence for God only, for my expectation is from Him" (Ps. 62.1).

In order to listen, one must be quiet. He must get rid of noise. And not just external noise—things around us that can distract our attention. He must still the internal noises as well—worries, fears, frustrations, and resentments which keep screaming at us and tend to drown out God's quiet voice.

When He does speak to us, what does God long to say? Two things, says the Psalmist (Ps. 62.11-12). He wants us to know that He is strong and also that He is loving. In other words, that He's big enough to take care of everything in our lives, and loving enough to want to do so.

God speaks. But He longs also to listen. Good Father that He is, He is eager to have His children bring to Him the things that are on their minds. All things, in fact: both the good and the bad, the joyful and the sad.

For the joys of our lives, when shared with our Lord, become multiplied. And the sadnesses, when spoken to Him, become divided.

**Questions:**

How often do you listen to God? How regularly do you speak to Him?

# Achieving Peak Performance: God's Word

*Ephesians 6.10-18*

If prayer is the air we Christians breathe in order to stay spiritually healthy, then the Bible, God's Word, is the food we eat.

A healthful, balanced diet of nutritious food is crucial to an athlete's performance. Food provides strength and gives energy. It helps to maintain stamina. Several years ago my son Dan and I took a bicycle trip along the Pacific coast of the United States. We pedaled from Canada to Mexico in 25 days. En route we ate four meals daily—two breakfasts, lunch, and a hearty dinner. I lost 15 pounds. I discovered that, under such grueling conditions, the food I ate was being turned directly into the power I needed to keep going.

Jesus describes God's Word as spiritual food. When we "eat" it—that is, read it and prayerfully apply it to our lives—it nourishes us and gives us strength to endure, come what may. Thus, to take God's promises and commands into the mouths of our souls, and to digest them fully into the core of our spirits, is vital. Without them we weaken spiritually; we starve ourselves. And, finally, die.

Jesus Himself set an example for us. Throughout His entire life He made it a practice to feed upon God's Word regularly. As a direct result, when He found Himself in the situation of being tempted by the devil, God's Word sprang immediately—yes, reflexively—to our Lord's mind. And the result? Even when His body had become weakened after the prolonged season of fasting in the desert, His spirit nonetheless remained vigorous. With a strong reply to the devil, "It is written…" (Matt. 4.4), He withstood the temptations and conquered the tempter.

Wise Christian athletes learn the importance of eating properly and eating enough. They must consume physical food, yes, but spiritual food, too. For they know that, lacking either of them, they'll never reach their peak performance.

### Challenge:

For the next seven days keep a record of how much you ingest spiritually. That is, how often you read and take to heart God's Word. Where necessary, improve your intake.

# Achieving Peak Performance:
# A Mentor

*Luke 6.40*

Several summers ago a huge crane was brought on campus and parked outside my window. Deftly the operator extended that 65-foot boom to its longest reach and began lifting heating units high onto the roof of the library building. Veteran truck driver that I am, I adored with wonder—and drooled.

During lunch, I went out to talk to that skilled operator. I asked: "Where did you learn to run that huge machine?" His dry response: "From watchin' the old-timers."

His next words arrested me: "I s'pose yer' one of them professors around here, huh? Well, let me tell you somethin'. You can have all the book-learnin' in the world about these machines, but the best teachin' comes from watchin' the old-timers do it."

He punctuated his comments: "Just watch the old-timers, young man. They'll learn you how."

Incorrect grammar. Wise advice.

Jesus did some of His teaching by the words He spoke. Mostly, however, He taught His disciples by His example. He *lived* the kingdom of God day by day. His disciples watched how He did it, and they began to imitate Him.

The best teaching, as every skilled teacher knows, is always done by modeling. Students begin to copy their finest teachers, wise friends whom they respect. They begin to do and say as they do and say. It's as simple—and as profound—as that.

We call these teachers "mentors." A mentor is an older, more mature, more experienced person who can help his pupils to "learn the ropes," so to speak. A good athletic mentor can mean the world to a younger athlete, of course, and make a lifetime of difference in how well she does.

In the same way, a skilled spiritual mentor can guide a younger Christian toward peak performance spiritually.

And can make an eternity of difference.

### Questions:

Who's teaching you the ropes as a Christian? If no one, by what reasonable time will you be able to ask an older, wiser Christian friend to mentor you?

# Encouraging One Another

*I Thessalonians 5.11*

The year 1999-2000 was a storybook season in Calvin College men's basketball—30-2 overall, undefeated in the league, and an NCAA Division III national championship. Our team had already accomplished by mid-season many of the goals it had set for itself. As coach, therefore, I had the enviable task of trying to help the team to reach even higher, to reset its sights, and to go for even more. At a team meeting, therefore, I gave each player a blank piece of paper and asked him to write out his additional personal goals and to dream of what contributions he could make to the team's further success.

Here's what Robby, whose severe foot injury had put him on the bench for the rest of season, wrote: "I will be a better encourager to my teammates and be a vocal leader."

What a gift to his teammates, and to the entire team! Instead of pouting or complaining about his own misfortune, he, an outstanding practice player in his own right, served as an encourager from the bench. He focused on what others could receive from him and not what he wanted for himself.

Persons like Robby don't get a lot written about them in the paper. Their stats don't deserve it—so the sports editors think. But from a coach's point of view, selfless encouragers like Robby deserve a standing ovation.

That is why at a dinner celebrating the winning of the national championship I asked the audience to give him one.

Encouragement is a great gift which athletes can give to one another. Christian athletes: Encourage. Encourage. Encourage. Never tire of doing so.

**Question:**

What is your "encouragement-quotient"?

# Team Chemistry

*I Thessalonians 3.2, Philippians 2.21-24*

" Team chemistry"—what an apt phrase to describe the magic that can happen. Gather a group of players together, teach them how to play together as a team, to care about and trust one another both on and off the field, to support one another to the max, and then watch what amazing things happen. The best way to describe the powerful impact and effect is to label it a chemical reaction.

A chemical reaction takes place when a number of separate elements, activated by a catalyst which ignites the process, join together to form a compound. The elements lose their separate identities. A new element comes into existence.

Team chemistry is a vital component to success in sports. Without it, a team of highly talented players never reaches its potential. It remains pathetically mediocre. When it's present, however, a team whose players have only average talent can beat players who are far superior.

For athletes who are followers of Jesus Christ, the call to live and play together as a team—to work toward team chemistry—has a special challenge. For time and again—no fewer than 32 times, in fact—the New Testament writers declare the Gospel's "one another" commands. Here are but a few: "*Welcome* one another" (Rom. 15.7); "*encourage* one another" (I Thess. 5.11); "*be patient with* one another" (Eph. 4.2); "*be humble toward and gentle with* one another" (Eph. 4.2);

"*pray for* one another" (I Thess. 5.25); "*be kind and compassionate to* one another, *forgiving* each other" (Eph. 4.32).

Imagine the power and magic that would be unleashed if players and coaches, trainers and fans—everyone—in fact, everyone world-wide—began to act toward one another in such a radically Christ-like manner.

**Questions:**

Which of these "one another" commands would build unity on your team? How will you live out that command?

# Coach

*I Thessalonians 5.12-13*

n *Love Beyond Reason,* John Ortberg describes Mrs. Beier, his child-hood piano teacher. An elderly German with not a trace of non-sense in her, "for five years she dominated the life of my family," recalls Ortberg.

Not that learning from her was sheer terror and drudgery. Quite the contrary. Because she herself could play so well, she got her pupils excited about playing and evoked from them a *desire* to play better. She challenged them, "If you'll trust me, if you will put yourself in my hands, if you'll do what I tell you to do, one day you'll be able to do what I do. One day the music will be in you."

Adds Ortberg: "Like every great teacher, what moved her to teach was love. Her love for music. Her love for her students. Truly great teaching is always a form of love."

So is great coaching. Most coaches aren't in it for what they can get out of it. Rather, they love the game; they love their students; and they love to teach.

But coaches, no matter whether veteran or young, need some-thing from their players in return. They need loyalty, respect, and trust. In short, players need to be teachable.

When a new coach comes on the scene, it's sometimes difficult for players to see the plan he has in mind for the team. Older players, remembering the approach of their previous coach, find it easy to mutter and complain, "We've never done it this way before." The result: other players begin to question and lose confidence.

St. Paul encourages Christians "to respect those who work hard among you, who are over you in the Lord and who admonish you. Hold them in the highest regard in love because of their work" (I Thess. 5.12-13).

Let Christian athletes on the team set the pace in doing so.

For, if great teaching is a form of love, so is being teachable.

### Challenge:

Inspect your attitude toward your coach. How well are you living up to the command in I Thessalonians 5.12-13?

# What Do We Owe Our Opponents?

*Matthew 5.43-48; I John 3.11-16*

Think right now of your arch-rival, the team that you most love to beat each season. In your deepest heart of hearts, what attitudes and thoughts do you cultivate toward these players and coaches? How *ought* you to think of them?

To think appropriately about and to act properly toward an opponent are tricky feats for a Christian. On the one hand, of course, you want to beat them—and beat them soundly. After all, they are arch-rivals of yours, and wanting to conquer them is the very stuff of which competition is made. On the other hand, as Christians we are commanded by our Lord Himself never to hate, but always to love. And to that command Jesus didn't add this qualifier: "except when playing your arch-rival."

So, what's a Christian to do? For starters, try on the following for size:

1. *Keep your spirit from doing little murders.*

Belittling, insulting, hating, or killing your opponent by your thoughts, words, looks, or gestures is to do a little murder on him. These spring from envy, anger, pride, and a desire for revenge. Thus, when you find these sprouting within you, with God's help, return to more healthy, more life-producing, more Christ-imitating attitudes and motives.

2. *Remember that it is not your opponent who determines how you're*

*going to act toward him or her. Only you can do that.*

You cannot control the attitudes, motives, and actions of another. You are, however, in charge of your own. Practice self-control and proper restraint toward your opponent, no matter how she might act toward you.

3. *Before you begin the game, remember what Jesus said and did.*

He gave the Golden Rule: "So in everything, do to others what you would have them do to you" (Matt. 7.12). He Himself lived what He preached.

4. *During the game be counter-culturally zany.*

Rather than talking trash to your opponent, be courteous and show him a concrete kindness.

5. *In both victory and defeat, be gracious.*

If you win, don't gloat. If you lose, be generous in praise of your opponent's success.

6. *In everything, keep your focus on the game itself.*

Keep hating to lose. Play hard—so very hard that if you're ever beaten, it won't be for lack of trying.

# Keepers of the Rules: Referees, Umpires, Line Judges, and the Rest

*Romans 12.16-21*

A good referee is something like a waterpipe under the street. Both perform important service, but ought not to be very obvious as they do so.

I'd find it hard to referee a game. When you do your job well, few people notice, and even fewer care enough to say thanks. And when you don't, many do notice and are quite ready to report your failings, both to you and to everyone else. They're eager to tell how good their eyes are compared to yours.

How should a Christian athlete relate to officials? Let me suggest a few attitudes, each of them in the spirit of Romans 12.16-21:

1. *Acknowledge their important role in the contest.*

A game wouldn't be a game without rules—and without someone to enforce them. When a referee blows a whistle and stops play, presumably it's to make right a wrong and to keep the participants playing fairly.

2. *Before game or match time, greet them with a warm welcome.*

Treat them as guests in your gym, on your court, or on your playing field. They've come to assist and serve you. Therefore, offer them your Christian hospitality—a smile, a handshake, an encouraging nod.

*3. Be patient with their failures.*

Even the best officials—and, let's admit it: Not all of them deserve the title best—even the best miss a call at times, or make one they shouldn't have. They blow it. But so do you at times.

Some coaches and players habitually express "referee rage." They constantly berate officials for poor calls. But Christian athletes and coaches ought not to. They ought to keep their cool.

The advice my grandmother once gave me is wise: "Before you speak, ask yourself: 'Is it true; is it necessary; is it kind?'"

*4. After the contest, say thanks.*

Honest gratitude is never out of place.

In summary, the writer of Ecclesiastes says that there is "a time to speak, and a time to keep silent" (Eccles. 3.7). Good words—in this case, toward an official—are "like apples of gold in a pitcher of silver" (Prov. 25.11). And as for bad words toward an official, consider the advice of Sirach: "There is a time in which he who keeps silent is wise."

# Fans and Other Spectators

*I Thessalonians 1.4-10*

L ike it or not, every time you put on your uniform and step onto the playing field, you are "on parade." You become a public person, and the people in the stands will be watching you. Be sure of this: They'll be watching a lot more than your play. They'll also be checking how you act. And from your actions, they'll be inferring some important things about you: who you are; for whom or what you are living and playing; and whether what you confess with your lips is consistent with how you behave.

To state the obvious: You are a witness. As a Christian athlete, you will by your decorum on the court either be commending the Lord Whom you profess to love and serve, or asserting His irrelevance to your life.

In I Thessalonians, Paul says about the infant Christians in the pagan city of Thessalonica that "the Lord's message rang out from you," and "your faith in God has become known everywhere" (I Thess. 1.8). Simply by the way they conducted themselves—how they spoke and what they did—these new believers were commending the Lord Who had rescued and saved them.

We Christian athletes would do well to imitate these early believers. So, here's a challenge. As you're suiting up for the game, ask yourself, "Will my speech and actions tonight serve to commend my Lord to these spectators who have come to watch me play?"

# Teamwork

*I Thessalonians 1.1-3*

S ays Lou Holtz: "When you get a group of people together, it's a start. When you get a group of people to stay together, it's progress. When you get a group of people to work together, it's success."

And that's teamwork.

But how does a group begin to work together—to become a team? To begin with, says Holtz, they learn to like one another. They appreciate one another for who each of them is, and they learn to enjoy one another's company.

These individuals must come to believe in one another, too. They must feel secure about who each of them is and appreciate the gifts that each of them has. If you feel confident about who you are, then you can begin to look for the good gifts in others, and to affirm them. By contrast, if you feel insecure about yourself and about your own role in the group, then you'll try to tear others down.

In this passage, notice how St. Paul—so obviously head and shoulders above Silas and Timothy—nonetheless includes them as equals in his greeting. In fact, later in the book he speaks so highly about Timothy, his pupil, that he calls him "our brother and God's co-worker" (I Thess. 3.2).

Compared to any individual member of it, team comes first. Always.

**Questions:**

Evaluate your own "team attitude":

1. Do you enjoy being with other team members?
2. How secure or insecure do you feel among them?
3. When is the last time you told another team member how much you value her or his presence on the team?

# God's Workmanship

*Ephesians 2.10, Philippians 4.4-8*

In my work as a college pastor I all too frequently come up against one vexing and sad problem: Many young people do not like who they are. Call it what you will—lack of self-esteem, insecurity, little-suicide syndrome, or whatever—the tragedy exists all the same. These people fail to appreciate their gifts. Compared to others, they feel themselves not very worthwhile. Thinking this way about themselves, they begin to shrivel up. They become a mere fraction of all that God intended them to be.

Persons with low self-esteem seem unable to look back upon few, if any, of their yesterdays with pride and pleasure. Nor do they seem to have much hope for their tomorrows. Day after weary and monotonous day they simply keep plodding along as one big disappointment to themselves.

How saddened I become whenever I meet a young person with low self-esteem. After all, this person has so much of his or her life ahead of them—a long string of days and years during which they could productively use the wonderful gifts they don't even believe they possess. Thus, if there were two gifts which—presto!—I could give to each of my young friends, I would long for them to know that:

1. *God, through Jesus Christ, calls them His beloved.* He loves and accepts them whoever they are and whatever they may have done or failed to do. He has forgiven their sad and sinful past and guarantees

them a future full of hope and promise.

2. *In Christ, each is a worthwhile person.* No matter how tattered and mixed-up each of us is—and all of us are—we have nonetheless been created by God and saved by Jesus for an important purpose.

How does one help another to know—really to know and *feel*—herself to be the gift that she actually is? By "worthwhiling" her, so to speak—pointing out the gifts she has and, then, encouraging her to use them to serve and enrich others.

Some people—coaches and players included—think it their task to keep others in their place, to humiliate and berate them.

Not so with Christian coaches and players. For Christians know that God has stamped each person with His image and loves her or him dearly.

And, therefore, coaches, players, and others ought to love them, too.

### Challenge:
Test your positive-quotient toward your coaches and teammates.

# I Can Resist Everything but Temptation

*James 1.12-16; 5.16*

When I was young, my parents taught me a song: "Oh be careful little eyes what you see. Oh be careful little tongue what you say. Oh be careful little ears what you hear. Oh be careful little feet where you go."

And why? "For the Father up above is looking down in love, so be careful little eyes what you see."

Not bad advice, I think, especially if you have really come to know how open to temptation each of us is, and how weak is our resistance.

Some people are quite impressed—*too* impressed, in my opinion—with human ability to resist temptation and to choose the right path over the wrong. By my reckoning, Oscar Wilde was a lot closer to the truth when he commented: "I can resist everything but temptation."

As athletes who strive to follow Christ, we need help to resist evil. We need God, and we need one another.

Before God's face, name your weakness. Be specific as you tell Him how weak you are. Then, plead for His help to withstand. Pledge, too, to steer wide and clear of any area where you are especially vulnerable.

Then search out another person or two who is unswervingly trustworthy. Be honest with him or her. Admit your weakness, and have them agree to hold you accountable.

Doing these two things, you'll be a more faithful follower of your Lord, both on and off the field. And you'll find yourself more and more committed to living a life that frustrates your tempter but pleases your Lord.

# Character Qualities: Joyful Gratitude

*II Corinthians 2.14*

I n his book *Authentic Christianity,* pastor and author Ray Stedman discerns five character qualities of a contagious, growing Christian. The apostle Paul lists them in his second letter to the Corinthian church (II Corinthians 2.14-3.6). We shall treat each of them in the next five meditations.

The first quality is gratitude. Paul says: "With thanks to God...." In the New Testament there is a close relationship between three words and concepts: grace *(charis)*, joy *(chara)*, and thanksgiving *(eucharistia)*. God's lavish goodness *(charis)* toward us produces joy *(chara)* within us, which, in turn, prompts us to give Him thanks *(eucharistia)*.

For this reason, a Christian who is living as God intends cannot be dull. She tries to stay alert to how good—how *immensely* good—the gift of her life really is, and how chock-full of undeserved blessings from God.

Ask any Christian person to spend even a mere five minutes purposefully identifying the numerous blessings God has showered upon her. When she's finished, she's certain to burst forth in thanksgiving and joyful praise.

To stay fully human and fully alive—spiritually trim and fit—a healthy Christian pays deliberate, careful attention to her life. For she is intent on spotting the goodnesses of God toward her. Once she has discovered them, she opens her mouth to give God deep and warm thanks. The exercise complete, she reminds herself—yet once again—that it is God who has given her all these good and wonderful things.

If you're an athlete who is striving to follow Jesus Christ, St. Paul has both an invitation and a command for you. Do look back, he says. Do a survey of the experiences you've had in your sports career—the fun-filled times with your teammates, the exciting games and matches, the good coaches. Be very specific. Start your sentences with "Remember the time when...." Such a command is easy to do, of course, for our lives are crammed so full of many good experiences that we hardly know where to begin.

Two additional commands flow from the first one. First, be joyful about them. Savor them for the *good* gifts that they really are. And, then, say thanks to God for them.

After all, it's the only right and fitting thing to do.

## Challenge:

Recall your best moment in sports. Think about it for several moments—how really good it was when it happened, and how much fun you had. Then, tell your story to a friend or to your entire team. Together give thanks to God.

# Character Qualities: Confident Trust

*II Corinthians 2.14*

The second character quality of a healthy, growing Christian is confident trust: "But thanks be to God, *Who always leads us in triumphal procession....*" The metaphor Paul uses here describes a parade through the streets to celebrate a military victory. It was the equivalent of a victory celebration in sports: bands playing, people yelling, banners, trophies carried high—the works.

Describing those who belong to Jesus, Paul says they are part of a victory parade—they're on the winning side. By His cross and resurrection, Jesus, their Lord, has won the battle. Once He was a victim, a sacrifice for sin. But no longer. Now He is victor. Best of all, His followers have a share in His victory and are entitled to join in the celebration.

Note one word in particular: *always.* Paul reminds us Christians that no matter what may happen to us—no matter what the circumstances of our life—we are always on the winning side. When the wind is at our backs, things are going well for us, and we're riding the wave of success in all that we do, then we're obviously on the winning side. But so, too, when nothing seems to be going our way. Even when the wind is in our faces, and we don't *feel* very victorious, we are, *in fact,* on the winning side. Because we belong to Jesus, our already victorious Lord, we simply cannot lose, come what may.

What radically good news this is! As athletes we know how quickly our fortunes can change. One day we're at the top of our game, and then—all of a sudden—things come crashing down. An injury or illness ends everything—our dreams, our season, or, even worse, our entire career. St. Paul reminds us that, since Christ is on our side—or, more correctly, since we are on His—He shall always—*always!*—lead us in triumph. What encouragement!

With Jesus the Victor as our Lord, we shall endure—and win! For, as Paul reminds us, "…neither death nor life, neither angels nor demons, neither the present nor the future, nor any powers, neither height nor depth, *nor anything else in all creation*, will be able to separate us from the love of God that is in Christ Jesus our Lord" (Rom. 8.38-39).

## Challenge:

Think of a person you know who, despite some rough circumstances, lived with a winning attitude because she or he belonged to Christ. Tell her or his story to your teammates.

# Character Qualities: Pleasant Scent

*II Corinthians 2.14*

Following upon the first two character qualities of a growing Christian (unquenchable joy and confident trust) and flowing out of them, the third quality Paul lists is *pleasant scent, good aroma* ("…and through us spreads everywhere the fragrance of the knowledge of Christ").

A healthy Christian emits a good odor. Her life is a sweet perfume.

Were you ever in a room with a detectible scent, a recognizable perfume? You knew you had smelled it somewhere before, but couldn't quite remember where or when? Finally, you recalled it: "Yes, it's *her* perfume. She always wears that kind." You then go on to assume: "She must have been here recently. Her perfume identifies her."

That's what St. Paul claims is true about Christians. They belong to Jesus Christ and are part of His victory parade. Now they have come to take on His pleasant aroma, His expensive perfume. Thus, wherever they go, they leave behind traces—unforgettable, clearly identifiable hints—of His pleasing and sweet odor.

One thing is certain about Jesus: When He lived here among us, people flocked to be near Him. Children and adults, rich people and poor, the powerful and the weak, fellow Jews and foreign Gentiles—everyone was magnetically attracted to Him. People "heard Him gladly" (Mark 12.37). The reason is obvious: He was a joy to be around. He emitted a pleasant odor. He was full of life—brimful—because He was filled with His Father's presence.

Jesus expects no less of His followers. Wouldn't it be tragic if Jesus, who is so attractive, became unattractive to people today because of the bad air, the disgusting smell, left by those who claim to be His followers?

**Questions:**

Analyze the perfume of your life: Are you an inviting advertisement for Jesus? Or does your smell drive others away?

# Character Qualities: Sincerity

*II Corinthians 2.17*

J ohn Ortberg (*Love Beyond Reason*) recalls the story about a man so desperate for work that he answered a zoo's want-ad for a man to imitate a gorilla. He got the job, donned the gorilla uniform, and began swinging back and forth in his cage.

One day the "gorilla" swung so hard on the rope that he ended up in the next-door cage. The lion's cage. Scared stiff, he ignored the disguise and screamed for help.

In response the lion charged up and yelled out: "Keep quiet, you idiot, or we'll both lose our jobs!"

How human beings—and Christians are not exempt—love to pretend! So easily and often they put on airs, acting on the outside what they're actually not on the inside. Thus they involve themselves in a duality of deceit. They lose their authenticity—and their integrity.

Take Moses, for example. When he came down from Mt. Sinai where God had met with him, his face was shining brilliantly with holiness. So brightly was he full of the presence of God that the people encouraged him to cover his face with a mask.

Gradually, however, the radiance began to fade away. But Moses did a deceitful thing: he kept putting on the mask before he went out in public. He acted as though he were something that in fact he was not. He wanted to appear more holy than he actually was.

If a big saint like Moses found himself so easily slipping into a pattern of deceit and inauthenticity, then how much more so do we. But it doesn't have to happen. When Christ dwells in us and we live by the power of His Spirit, then "in Christ we speak before God with sincerity" (II Cor. 2.17).

How does one keep from slipping into inauthenticity? By depending upon God daily for strength. Doing so, we can actually increase our level of reflecting God's glory, not decrease it, as Moses did (II Cor. 3.18).

As Christian athletes, we have an important opportunity, both on and off the court or playing field, to re-present our Lord. But to do so well requires a ferocious commitment to integrity and authenticity.

Thus, I challenge you to not "play games" with being a Christian. Be real. Remember the advice of the old Southern preacher: "Be what you is, 'cause if you is what you ain't, then you ain't what you is!"

**Challenge**:

Identify an area of your life that needs more authenticity. Pray for wisdom to initiate a plan to improve it and for strength to carry it out.

# Character Qualities:
# Open Letter, Winsome Advertisement

*II Corinthians 3.1-6*

We have discussed four character qualities of a maturing Christian, as Paul describes them in II Corinthians 2: joyful gratitude, confident trust, pleasant (Christ-like) aroma, and undeniable authenticity. In Chapter 3, Paul presents his fifth, his final, one: he compares a growing follower of Jesus to a letter of recommendation.

Anyone looking for a job knows how valuable a letter of reference can be. If it's a solid recommendation and is written by a reputable, distinguished person, it's like money in the bank.

Paul claims that by their very lives and speech the Corinthian believers are a strong letter of recommendation for the Gospel. They are a compelling, winsome advertisement. By reading the letter of these Christians' lives, others must conclude that the Good News of Jesus Christ is true.

This "letter" of recommendation is unique, claims Paul. In the first place, it is Jesus Christ Himself who is its author. He inscribed His message on these Corinthian Christians' lives.

Nor did Jesus use some ordinary ink when He composed it. He used the very "Spirit of the living God" Himself. Christ's Spirit is the means by which others read what He wrote.

Finally, note to whom this letter is addressed. Christ sends it to everyone. He intends it to be "known and read by everybody."

What an amazing metaphor: Christ longs to use our lives to serve as His letter of recommendation.

But it's more than just a metaphor. It's actual. The only description some people will ever have about Jesus—the only letter they will read about Him—is the letter of our lives.

May we all describe our Lord faithfully and well—in His wonderful grandeur and glory.

### Question:
What (or whom) does your life advertise?

# In a Slump

*II Peter 1.1-11*

I t happens even to the best of athletes: Strangely, mysteriously they get into a slump.

A similar thing can happen in the spiritual life. There can be long stretches in a Christian's journey when one's awareness of God is vivid and real. He feels so warm and embracing, so caring and nearby, that one thinks it would be impossible ever to doubt His presence and His power again.

But then comes a spiritual dry spell. It might creep into one's mind and heart ever so quietly and gradually, but the symptoms are unmistakable. God begins to feel distant. Prayer to Him seems like a pre-recorded message. Worship becomes more of a grim duty than an inviting delight. Times of spiritual intimacy become rare. Scripture's promises and commands no longer nourish one's soul—they're just words on a page. It feels as if you're only going through the motions of ritual.

Ancient writers call this spiritual slump *acedia*, sloth. It was so prominent, in fact, and happened to so many people, that they listed it as one of the seven deadly sins.

In his second letter, St. Peter was writing to early Christians who were in something of a spiritual slump. Notice how Peter sets about assisting them. First, he reminds them about what is true, no matter how they now may be feeling. He tells them that "through the righteousness of our God and Savior Jesus Christ" each of them has "received a faith as precious as ours." What is more, he reassures them that God's "divine power has given us everything we need for life and godliness...."

Then Peter looks toward their future. He assures them that—yes—they will make it out of their slump. "You will receive a rich welcome into the eternal kingdom of our Lord and Savior Jesus Christ."

Peter encourages them to keep up the right spiritual exercises: "For this very reason, make every effort to add to your faith...." In other words, don't become too upset with yourself. Don't focus too much of your mind and energy upon the slump itself. That only makes matters worse. Instead, quietly and gently—not forcefully—allow God's Spirit to remind you daily of His promises to you in Christ. Be reminded, too, that eventually your spirit will come out of the dark depths and sing in the light again.

Finally, Peter advises Christians in a slump to keep on practicing the spiritual exercises. Practice, practice, practice. Practicing the virtues will cause Christians to grow and flourish with each opportunity. If they do, then gradually they'll come out of their slump and regain their spiritual stride.

And that's for sure.

### Challenge:

1. What spiritual exercises keep you connected to God?
2. Find a scripture passage that declares one of God's promises to you. Memorize it now so that you can claim it the next time you are in a spiritual slump.

# When We Don't Succeed

*I Corinthians 4.2; Matthew 25.31-40*

In sports as in life, including the spiritual life, it's important to distinguish between faithfulness and success. As a Christian, I am called to the former, but not to the latter. In other words, I am called to do as well as I can, to put forth my very best effort. But I am *not* required to make sure that things turn out right, to always be successful.

Sometimes, despite my best efforts, failure happens. And that's OK. Simply that I was faithful in trying is enough.

I am always struck by Jesus' description of what will happen "when the Son of Man comes in His glory" and when God wraps up history. He, the great and final Judge, will divide people into appropriate groups. Some He will place at His right hand, and others He will send off to His left. And He will do this on the basis of what they've done with their lives, whether they've tried to help others or not.

Jesus gives some examples of how to help others: "I was hungry and you gave Me something to eat, I was thirsty and you gave Me something to drink, I was a stranger and you invited Me in…."

If you look carefully at most of these examples, says Fr. Isaias Powers (*Kitchen Table Christianity*), they're "success stories." A need was present—hunger, thirst, homelessness, nakedness—and the need was met.

Until you come to the last example: "I was in prison and you came to visit Me." Based upon how well things turned out in the previous five instances, I would have expected the last one to end something like: "…and you got Me out. You were successful in rescuing Me."

Not so, however. Jesus simply says: "…and you *visited* Me." That is, even though nothing much changed, you yourself did as well as you could.

How freeing this can be for an athlete and a coach. Others may harshly insist that you be successful—that you most definitely win the game, capture the league championship, go on to conquer the national crown.

Those who insist on success, of course, seem never to be satisfied with your present performance and accomplishments. They'll always keep raising the bar on you, and demand more success. And still more.

But Jesus calls us all to live by grace. "It doesn't bother Me that you're not always successful," He says to us. "Simply that you were *faithful*—that you did as well as you could—is a wonderful delight to Me."

And that, to be sure, is *very* liberating news for us all.

### Questions:

How can you put the importance of winning beneath being faithful? Would being more faithful in your athletic and spiritual training help?

# When We've Done Wrong

*I Corinthians 15.10*

John Ortberg in *Love Beyond Reason* recalls the time he went golfing with several friends. Having teed up for his first shot, he sliced it off at a hopeless and chaotic angle. His friends advised: "Take a mulligan."

A mulligan in golf is a second chance. You act as if the previous shot doesn't count, as though it never happened.

"Taking a mulligan" is an apt metaphor to describe what forgiveness is all about.

We are, each of us, evil people. Continually we tilt toward doing wrong, and not right. No matter how polite and "nice" we may appear on the outside, in the core of our beings—the Bible calls this center our "heart"—we are sick and sinful. So evil we are that if our deepest secret were ever to become known, each of us would be tempted to suicide for shame.

What is even more humiliating is the fact that we cannot get rid of this evil by ourselves. It is deep and indelible. Jeremiah the prophet asks, rhetorically: "Can the Ethiopian change his skin or the leopard its spots? Neither can you do good, [you] who are accustomed to doing evil" (Jer. 13.23). He adds: "The heart is deceitful above all things and beyond cure. Who can understand it?" (Jer. 17.9).

Only God can wipe away our past and give us a fresh start. John, the apostle of Jesus, calls us to remember that "If we confess our sins,

God is faithful and just to forgive us our sins, and to cleanse us from all unrighteousness" (I John 1.9).

How does this happen? It begins with our becoming sad about what we've done wrong. Really sad. (You understand, of course, that there's a big difference between remorse—feeling sorry that you've gotten caught, or might be caught—versus being genuinely sad and contrite.)

Then, we must come to God in penitence. Offering no excuses for what we've done, we honestly admit our wrong and plead His mercy.

When these two things happen, then—wonder of wonders—we hear God saying to us: "Because of my Son, Jesus Christ, I forgive you. What you've done wrong doesn't count anymore."

Then God does one more thing for us. He says: "Now you forgive yourself, too." In other words, don't keep clobbering yourself with how you've messed up. Give yourself a fresh start.

Take a mulligan.

### Challenge:

Reach deep into your heart and ask God to wash away your sins. Next, forgive yourself and experience a fresh start.

# Forgiving Others

*Matthew 6.14-15*

How do you handle someone who has hurt you? And did so not in a slight way—not a mere irritation or annoyance, like forgetting your name or denting your car—but very deeply. So deeply and seriously, in fact, that you just can't get out of your mind what he did. Every time you recall this affront, you experience anger and bitterness all over again.

Some people try to get over their hurts by pretending that nothing happened. Others give the one who hurt them a cold shoulder, freeze them out. (Silence toward another is, of course, a subtle and powerful form of revenge.) Still others try a more vigorous and overt revenge: they wallop the other person back.

But neither shutting another person out nor shouting him down gets rid of the problem. The cycle of violence not only continues, but it gets progressively worse.

Jesus advises that the only way to end the trouble between persons is to apply the salve of forgiveness. That way is to give the one who hurt you a fresh start, no matter how badly he hurt you and regardless of whether or not he deserves it.

Forgiving another is by no means easy. In fact, it's hard work. It's so hard, in fact, that without God's help, it can never happen. Forgiving, says Lewis Smedes (*Forgive and Forget*), begins by your taking the measure of how much the other person has damaged you—and how very deeply you hurt as a result. Quite possibly you're angry, too, and filled with hatred about the matter. That, too, needs to be faced head-on. But, then, after that, you resolutely, and with God's help, take the next huge step: you set your mind and heart on letting him off the hook. You determine to give him a fresh start, despite the fact that he doesn't deserve it.

Forgiving another is acting toward him as though the wrong he did toward you never happened.

Jesus doesn't merely advise us to forgive others when they wrong us. He *commands* us to. If we don't, He says, then God won't forgive us (Matt. 6.15, 18.35). Anyone who pleads for mercy from God is then pledged to show that same mercy to others.

However hard it may be to do so, to forgive is also good for our own spirits. Unless we do, we'll keep dredging up the hurts that others have done to us. Even psychologists tell us that savoring our hurts drains our spirits.

So give the other guy a mulligan—give him a fresh start by forgiving him. When you do, you'll be giving yourself one, too.

### Questions:

Who has hurt you badly? To what degree have you forgiven him or her?

# Facing Our Fears

*Joshua 1.1-11*

The land of Egypt lay behind them and fierce giants were ahead of them. To complicate matters, Moses, Israel's leader, the one who had rescued them from Pharaoh's oppression in Egypt and had delivered God's will to them at Mt. Sinai—this great and charismatic founder of their nation, had just died.

Israel was scared stiff. Behind those first words in Joshua 1, "Now Moses my servant is dead," lies a mountain of forboding and paralyzing fear. What to do when there's nothing to do?

Every athlete can recall a time when she or he has felt like those Israelites. The moment you stepped onto the opposing team's home floor, in your very gut you could *feel* how heavily the odds were against you. Their fans were raucous, rude, and hostile. The gym was poorly lit and a bear for visiting teams to get used to. Moreover, the other team always plays very well at home. As you weighed all this, fear began to creep into your soul. Your mouth felt like sawdust and your knees became watery.

What to do when we're afraid? Well, to begin with: Admit it. Some people prefer to pretend. They're all wound up on the inside, but on the outside they try to act as though nothing's wrong. They bluster.

But this doesn't work. Fear is always bigger than our ability to pretend. Sooner or later, it catches up with a swaggerer and wallops him.

So, admit that you're afraid. And, then, perhaps with your team-mates' and coaches' help, try to analyze what you're afraid of. Be specific in this; it will tend to "de-fang" some of the dread you feel.

Finally, learn to listen to the encouraging, fear-killing promises of God. As Joshua was about to succeed Moses—no small task!—and to lead the people in battle, the Lord came to him with these reassuring words: "As I was with Moses, so I will be with you. Therefore, do not be afraid."

God is with us, no matter what we confront. And He will never leave us to face our troubles alone.

Never.

**Questions:**
> What fear(s) are you confronting? How are you responding to them? To what degree are you depending on God for courage?

# Paranoia in Reverse

*Psalm 27*

hilip Yancey visited a number of Eastern European countries during the summer of 1991, soon after the fall of the Berlin Wall and the collapse of communism. Wherever he went, he met with groups of Christians who were joyous about regaining their freedom. They told him, too, about their endurance when their lives were threatened and their faith was under fire. They had been filled with fear. They had tended to become paranoiac.

In rapid-fire succession, the communists had imposed one repressive measure after another upon these believers. They forbade Christians to meet together. They prohibited them from printing articles in newspapers. They traced telephone calls—to name but a few of these restrictions.

At first the Christians responded in cat-and-mouse fashion. They met in secret. They faked authorship for printed articles. They called from public telephones. But despite these clever counter-measures, fear kept tying them up in knots. Though they remained free externally, fear gripped them from within.

So these Christians planned a new strategy. "Let's quit playing sneaky games with our tormentors," they said to themselves and to one another. "Let's take Jesus at His word—quite literally—when He assures us that we simply *cannot* lose, no matter what. We'll trust His promise that He will be with us, and that we need not fear anything or anybody."

So they did, and here's what happened: The communists rounded these Christians up in wholesale fashion, cracked their heads with clubs, beat their bodies mercilessly, and tossed them into prison.

But the Christians refused to budge. They kept believing Jesus' words. And the final result was this: though their bodies were being held captive, their spirits were free as a bird. Trusting fully that Jesus would do as He said, their fear dissipated.

Hearing these reports from his now-fearless East European Christian brothers and sisters led Yancey to a new definition of trust and faith. While a paranoiac person anxiously organizes her entire future around fear—around what might happen—a faith-filled person views her tomorrows through the lens filter of trust in God. Thus, concludes Yancey, faith is actually paranoia in reverse.

That's not a bad definition for Christian athletes to remember when they face fears bigger than their ability, on their own, to handle.

## Challenge:

As you and your team face the next big challenge, remember Christ's presence and power. Say to one another, "Paranoia in reverse!"

# Keeping in Shape

*I Corinthians 9.24-27*

The best way to get into shape is to never get out of shape. In other words, exercise always. Maintain a regular program of calisthenics so that your body is fully prepared, when it must, to respond to grueling activity. Stamina becomes developed over time, not overnight.

The same holds true spiritually. Two key ingredients to spiritual growth are time and exercise. Daily we must read and meditate upon God's Word. And not only daily, but from moment to moment, we must strive to keep applying that Word to our lives. We must keep obeying its commands and receiving its promises throughout the day as we face the multitude of situations that happen to us. As we maintain this regimen and depend constantly upon our Lord for strength to do so, we will over time develop spiritual stamina.

But slack off, however briefly, and one thing is certain to happen: we'll soon be out of shape. We'll lose tone in our spiritual muscle and quickly become winded, so to speak.

Stay in spiritual shape always.

And never get out of it.

**Question:**

What is your spiritual training regimen?

# No Instant Success

*Hebrews 11.13-16*

Nobody—absolutely nobody—becomes a strong athlete overnight. Developing athletic prowess and skill takes days and
years of practice. And then still more practice. Even the most
skilled superstar keeps drilling in the fundamentals. Without the
practice, you lose your touch. You stop improving. And then you lose
ground.

So, too, in the Christian life. There simply are no instant saints.
A disciple of Jesus is an apprentice, and apprentices improve their
skills only gradually. Apprentices try, and they sometimes fail. They
fail very often at first. But they don't quit. They keep trying until
they've completely mastered what they're learning.

No apprentice of Jesus ever becomes so skilled that he outgrows
his need to keep practicing the virtues which Jesus Christ, his Master,
is teaching him. The more he obeys the teachings of his Lord, the
more he grows in faithfulness and in spiritual maturity.

In one notable respect, however, a spiritual learner differs from a
physical one. Physical athletes gradually reach their peak, and then
decline. Their hand-eye coordination declines; their reflex time slows;
their entire body weakens in strength. Eventually they must retire.

Not so in the spiritual life. A person can keep growing—he must
do so, in fact—for the rest of his days on earth. The longer he lives,

the more he can grow in likeness to his Lord. He never ceases to pursue the quest for holiness, for it is a quest that never ends.

A centuries-old Christian confession declares, "In this life, even the holiest [people] have only a small beginning of [Christian] obedience. Nevertheless, with all seriousness of purpose [that is, "with practice"] they do begin to live according to all, not only some, of God's commandments."

After years and years of striving to stay in step with Christ and to obey Him carefully, a wise and elderly Christian saint once commented, "The Christian life is a matter of walking, falling down, getting up again, and then keeping on going."

And keeping on doing so for the rest of one's life, as we said earlier. Until we see Jesus.

## Challenge:

One of my favorite quotes about training is, "Either you get better or worse; you never stay the same." How does this apply to your life both athletically and spiritually?

# Declaration of Dependence

*Psalm 46*

I f they're honest, athletes and coaches who become successful and gain fame admit they didn't get where they are by themselves. They're generous in crediting others.

In June, 2000, Denver Christian's Dick Katte, the winningest basketball coach in Colorado's history (646–157, with five state championships, four runners-up, and 18 Metropolitan League titles) was the first to receive the Dave Sanders Award. Sanders was the 25-year teacher-coach who died in the Columbine, Colorado, high school massacre in 1999. The prestigious award was established to recognize "the Colorado coach who best exemplifies Sanders' qualities of commitment, courage, and teaching skills to Colorado student athletes."

It was no small honor for Katte to be the first chosen for this award. But here's what he said upon receiving it: "You can't do this without great people, great family, and the grace of God. It's a combination of things."

In the Christian life, too, no maturing saint is so foolish as to think she's grown spiritually by herself. She graciously acknowledges the support of the many people who in various ways have assisted her. Gladly and generously, of course, she gives thanks to her God Who ultimately makes such progress possible. There is no room for self-centered bragging. What is called for is a generous appreciation for all those who have made her growth possible.

Such a declaration of dependence upon God and others can actually increase the joy and confidence of living. It can make us more grateful when things in life go well for us, more patient when they don't, and more confident regarding our future. For we know that, come what may, we belong to a God Who is shaping our tomorrows for His glory and for our welfare.

"God is our refuge and our strength"—yes. But to become aware of that means paying deliberate and careful attention to this great truth. Daily, therefore, at day's beginning, we do well to pause and reflect upon God's call to us: "Be still, and know that I am God."

And then to remember: "The Lord of hosts is with [me], the God of Jacob is [my] refuge."

**Prayer:**

"May Your unfailing love rest upon us, O Lord, even as we put our hope in You." (Psalm 33.22)

# "I Played for My Father"

*Psalm 115.1*

C huck Swindoll tells the story of a college football player who didn't get much playing time. But there were reasons. His heart just wasn't in the game. He ignored the training program, had to drag himself to practice, and went through the drills only half-heartedly. As a result, he mainly sat the bench. His position on the team, says Swindoll, was "somewhere between being on the bench and off the team."

During practice one day the young man got an emergency message from home. It came from his mother. The coach delivered it to the young fellow, and he read it. It said, "Your father died this morning. Take next plane home. (Signed) Mom."

The fellow gathered with his family at home. Together they buried his father. Sometime thereafter he returned to school and rejoined the team.

Prior to the next game—a big one against the school's arch-rival—the young man asked his coach to let him start. The coach refused. But as the game progressed, the home team started to fall behind—badly. The young fellow asked the coach again, "Put me in, please. Let me play."

Finally the coach did. To everyone's surprise, the young man played well—very well. Several times he broke through the defensive line for some good yardage. He even caught a touchdown pass.

The third and fourth quarters went like the first two. The young man played as if he were out of his mind. There was fire in his eyes and adrenalin in his veins. He was determined. He played his heart out—left everything on the field, so to speak.

The home team did end up losing. But when the players huddled in the locker room and the coach stepped in to debrief them, he turned to his usually bench-sitting player and asked, "Son, whatever got into you today that you played so well?"

Here's what the young fellow replied: "Coach, when my father was alive, he was blind, and was never able to see me play. But today, for the first time, he was watching me. And I played for him."

Christian athletes: God our Heavenly Father is not blind, of course. Quite the contrary. His eyes are continually on us when we play. And His face shines with delight when we give Him our best— when we play especially for Him.

And so, with this prayer on our lips, we offer Him our athletic skills and, indeed, our entire lives: "Not to us, O Lord, not to us, but to Your name be the glory, because of Your steadfast love and faithfulness."

## Challenge:

In your next athletic contest—practice or game—think, with joy, about your Father watching you.

# Index of Scripture Passages